This Book Belongs To:

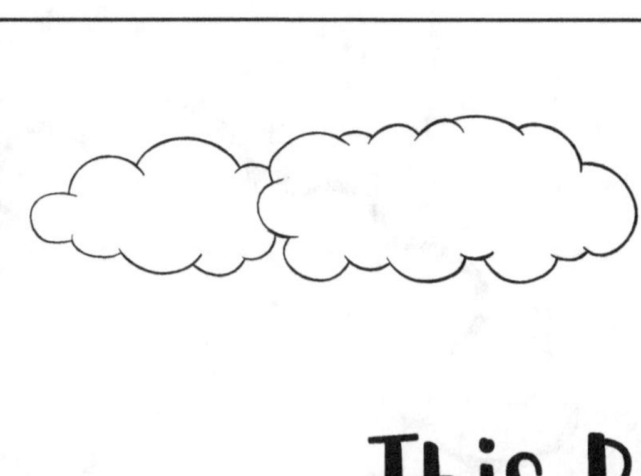

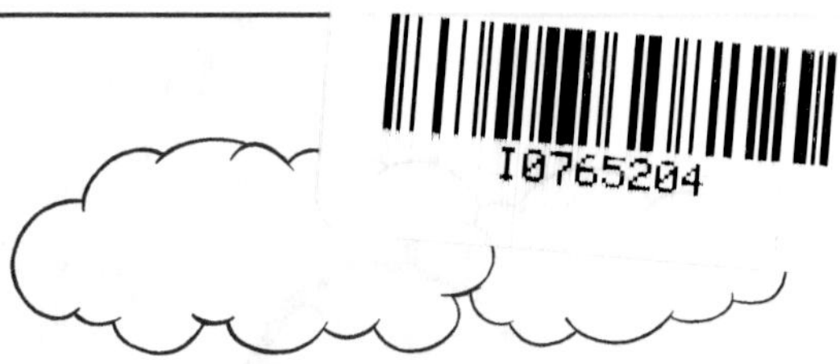

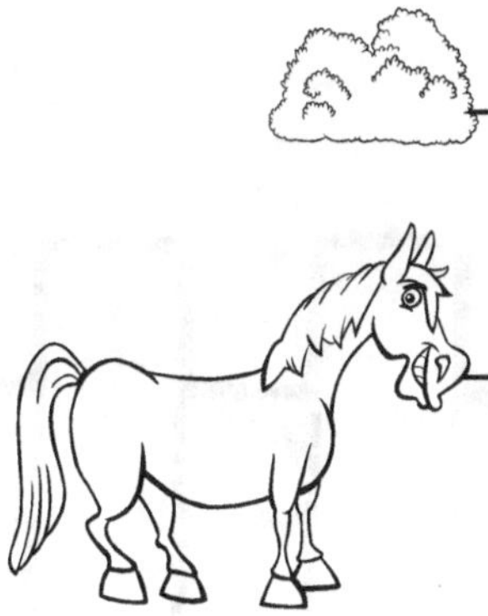

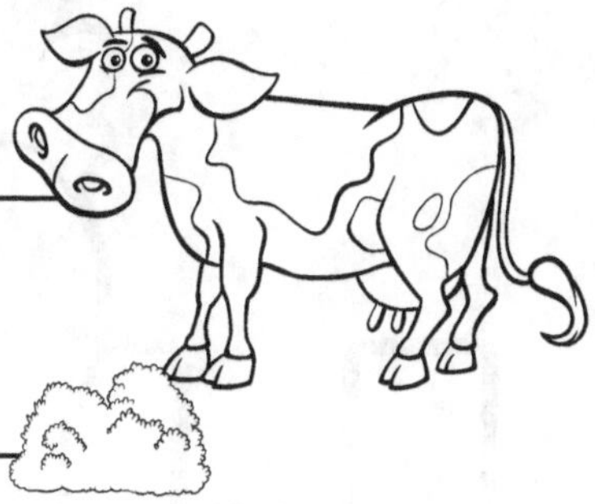

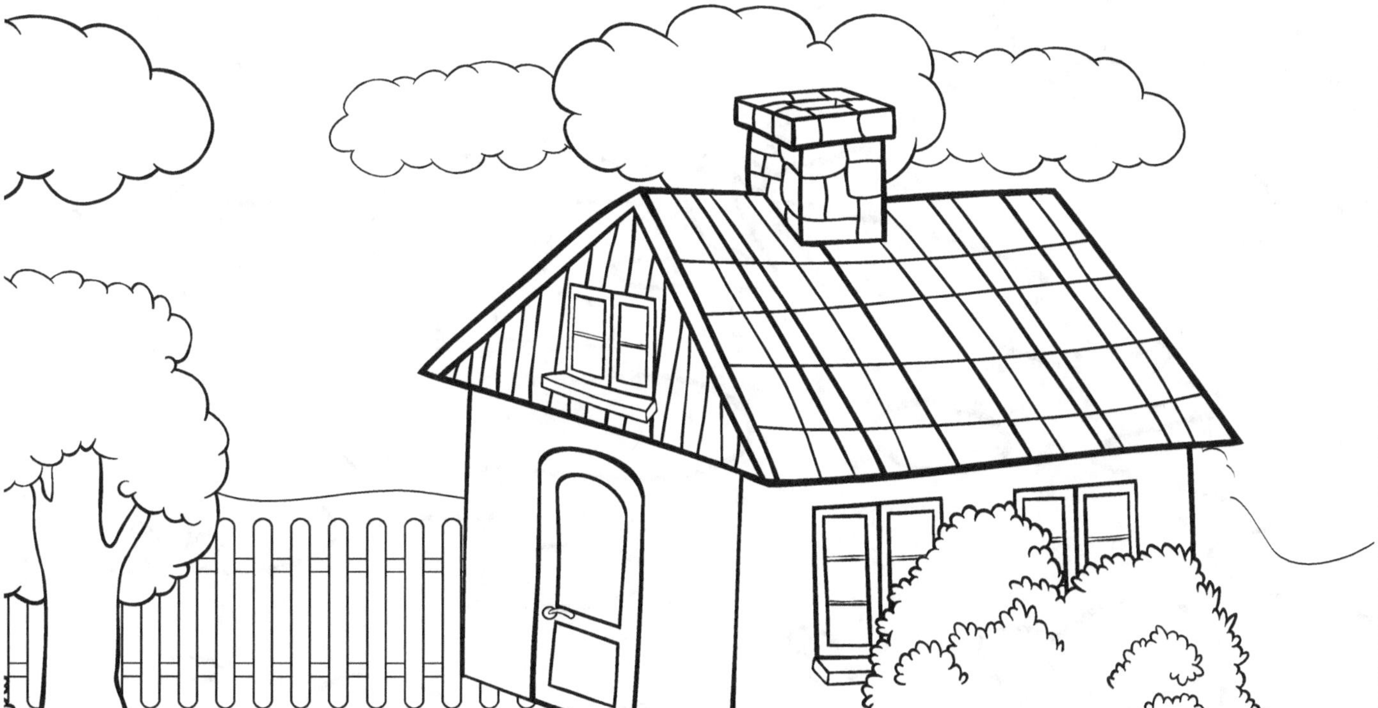

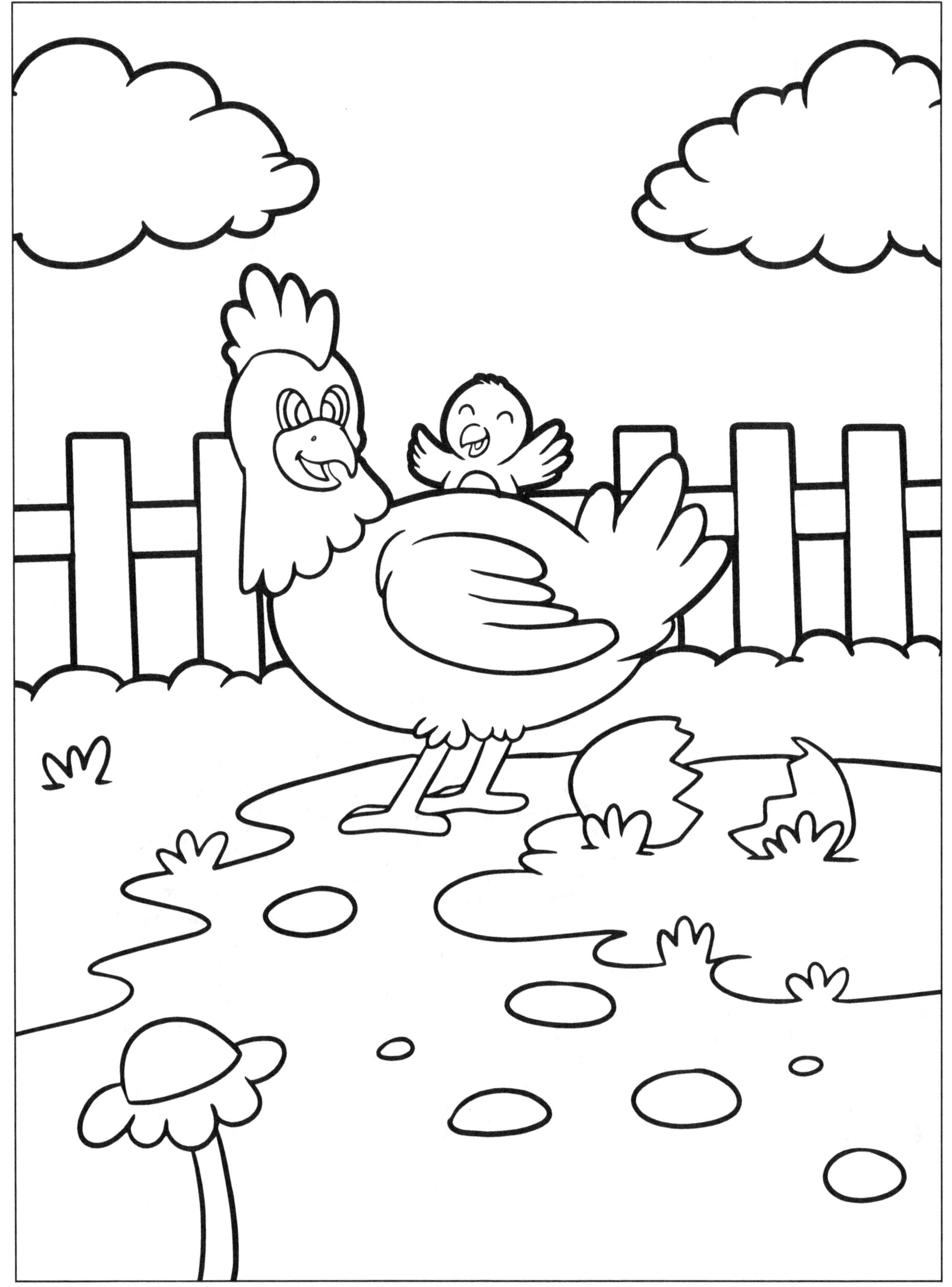

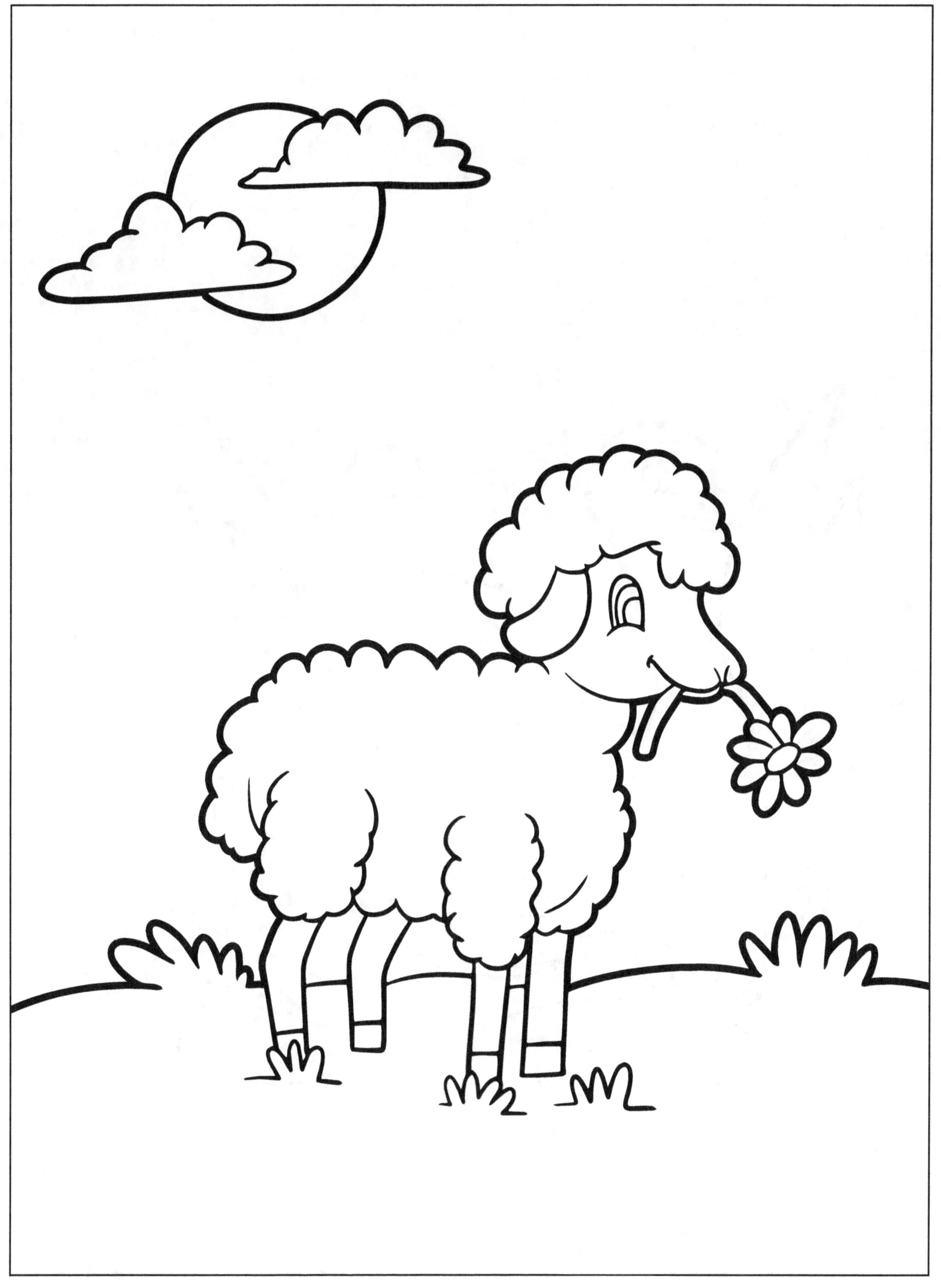

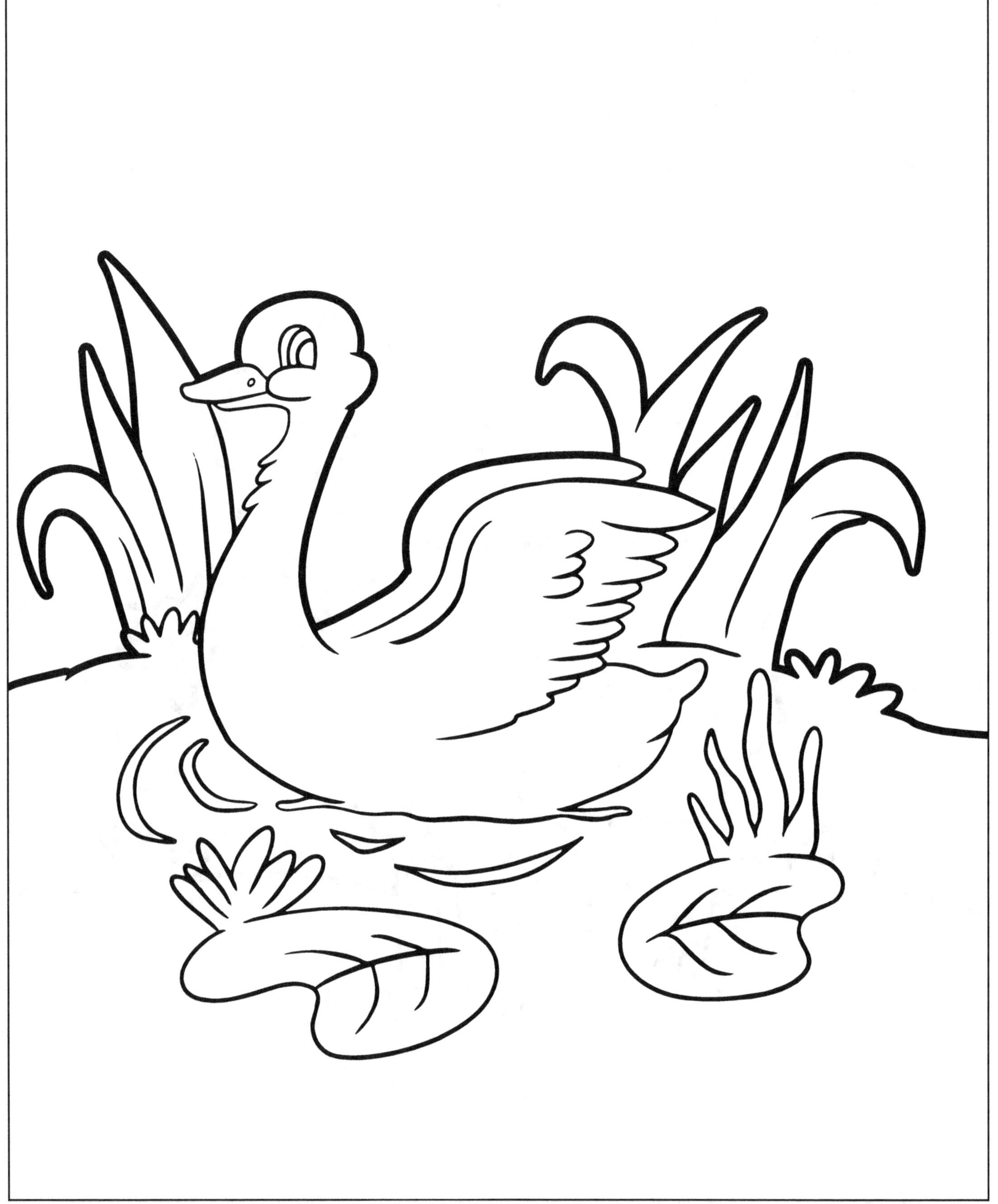

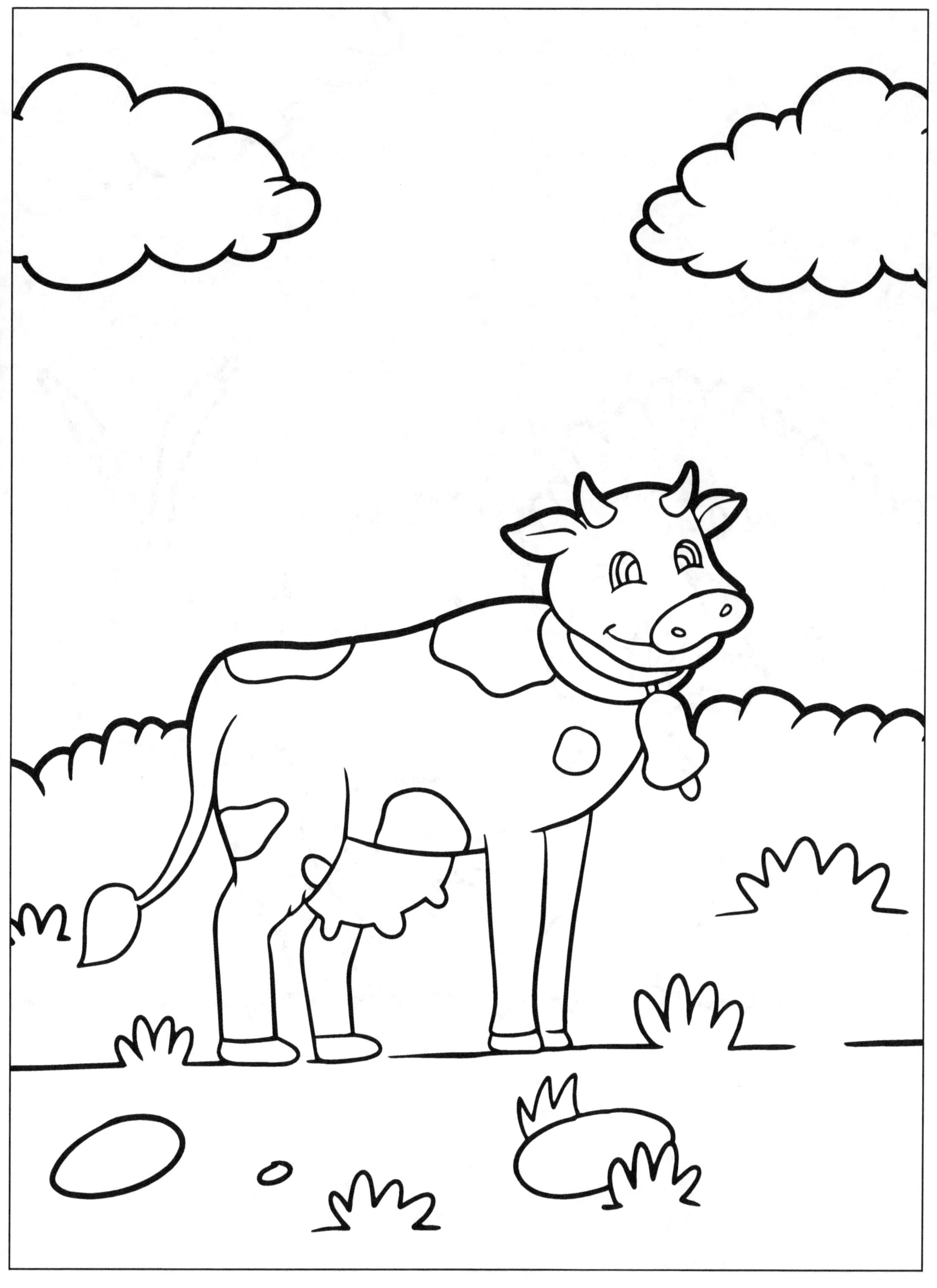

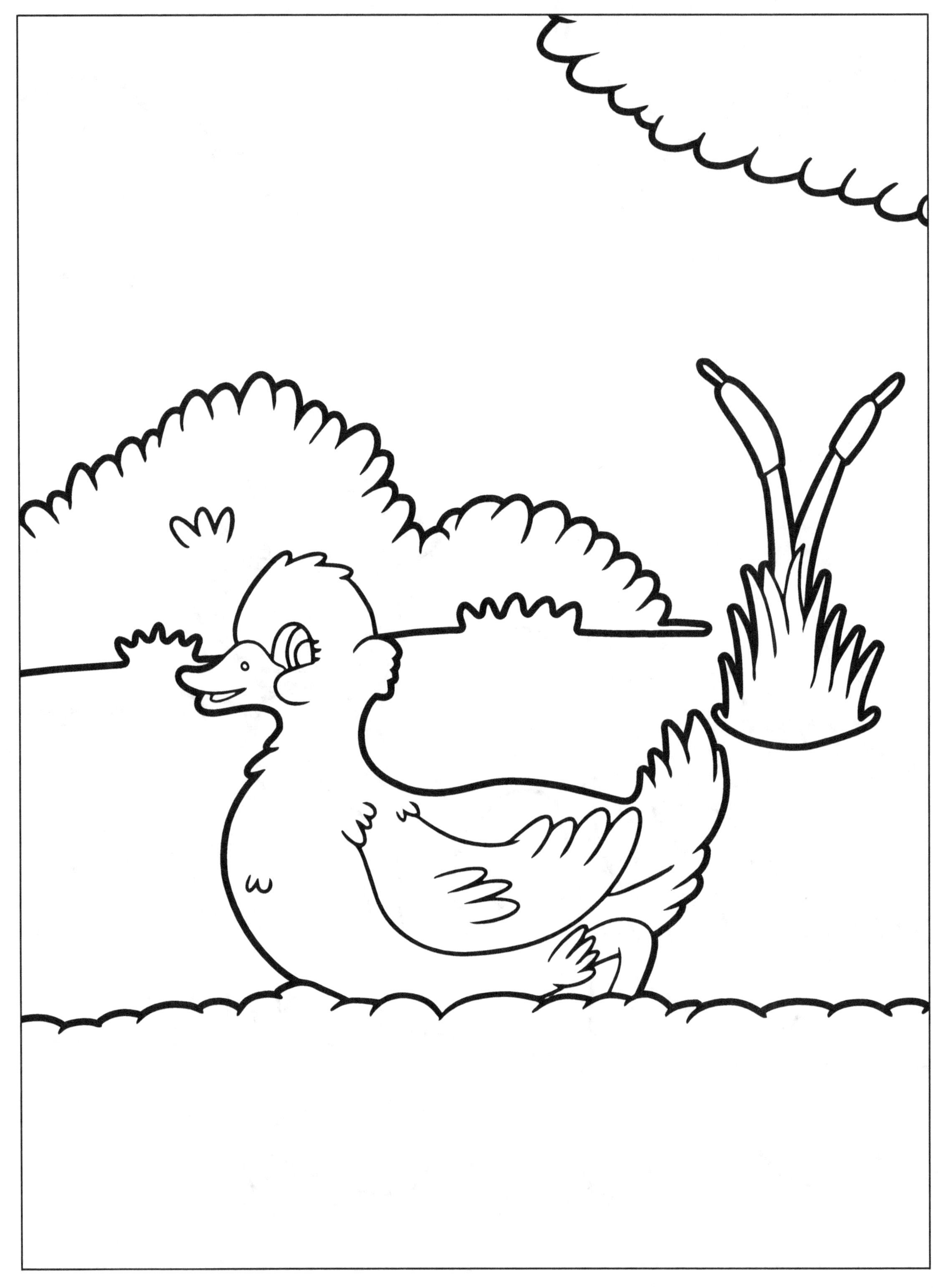

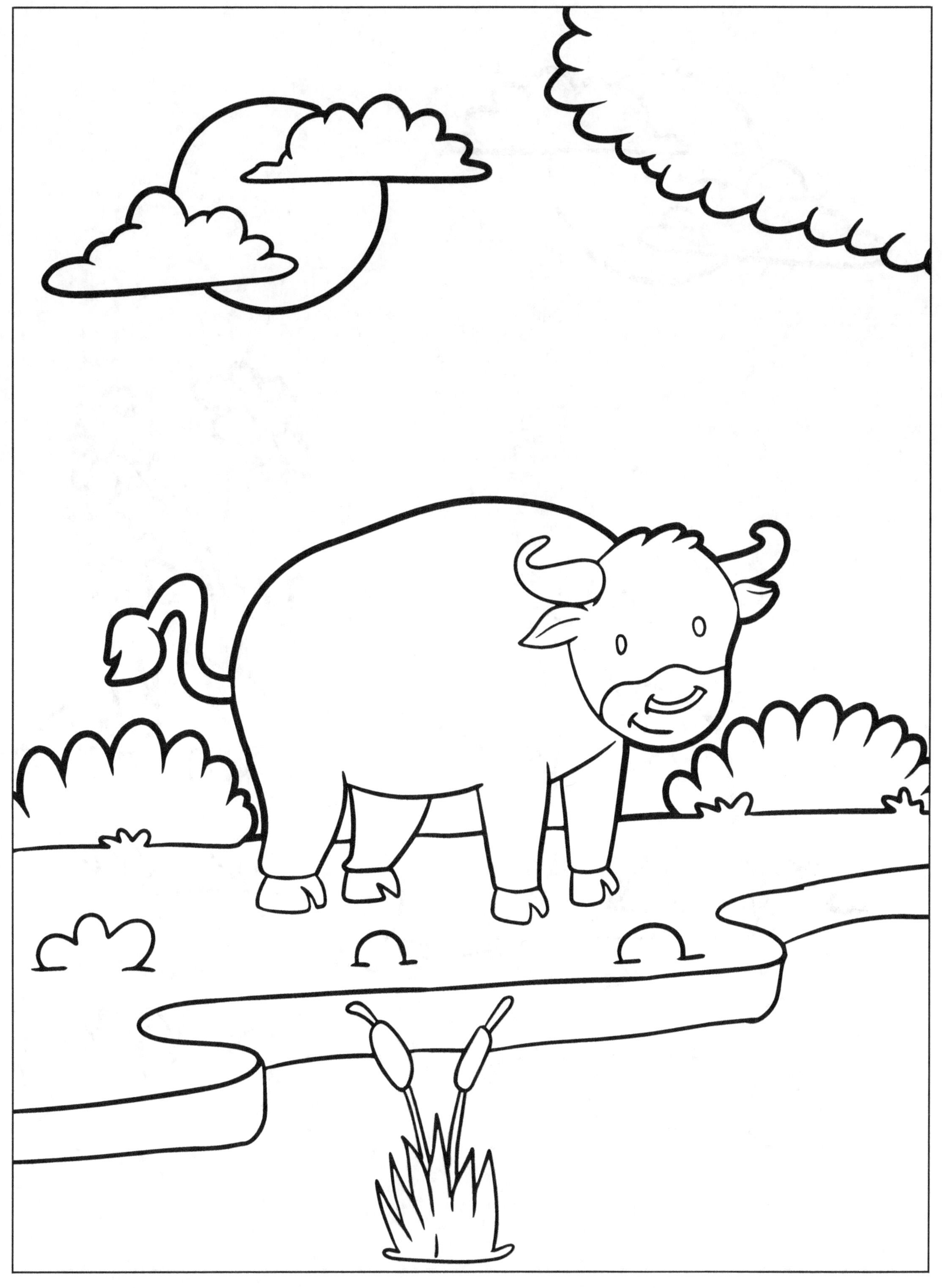

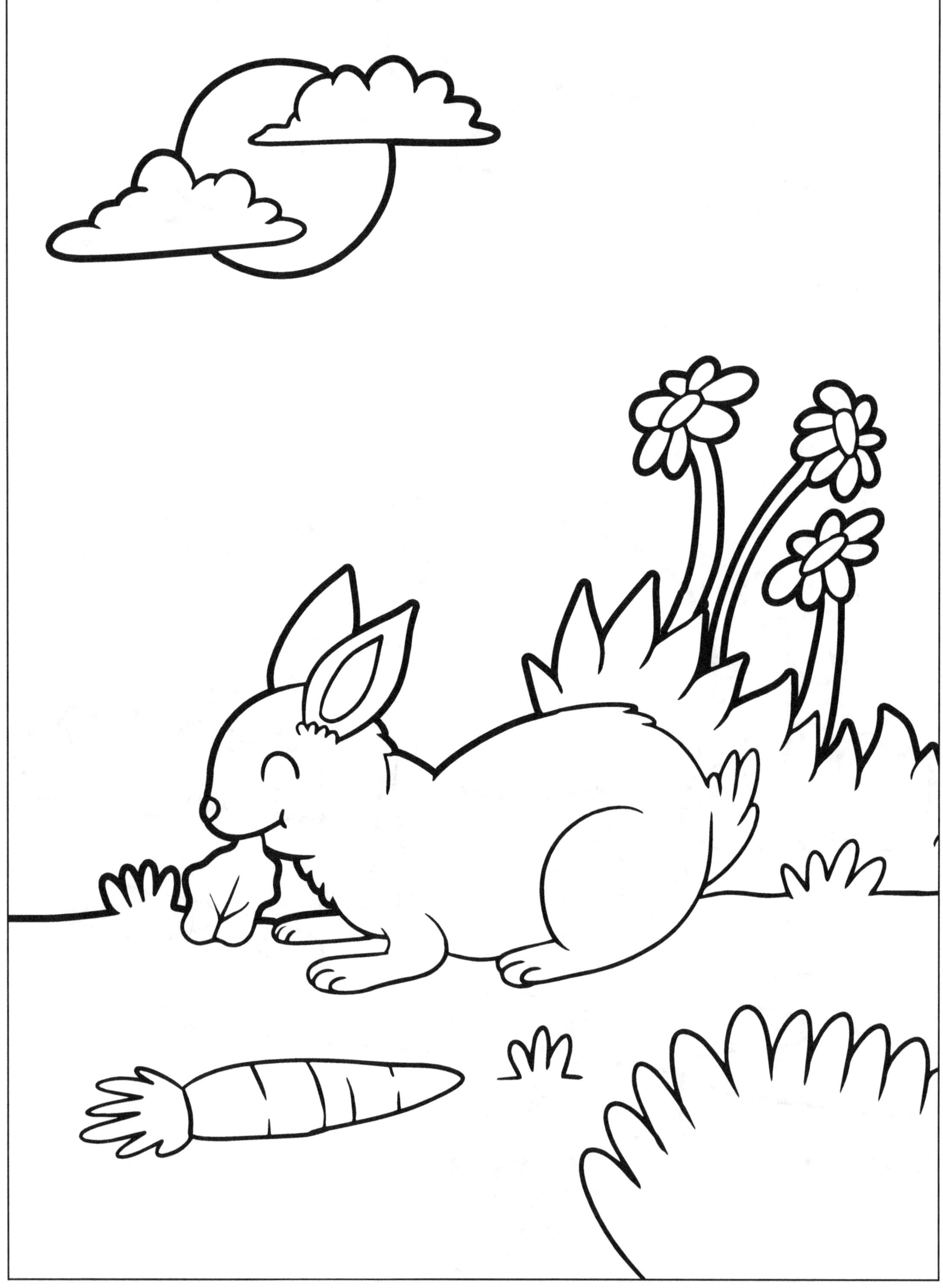

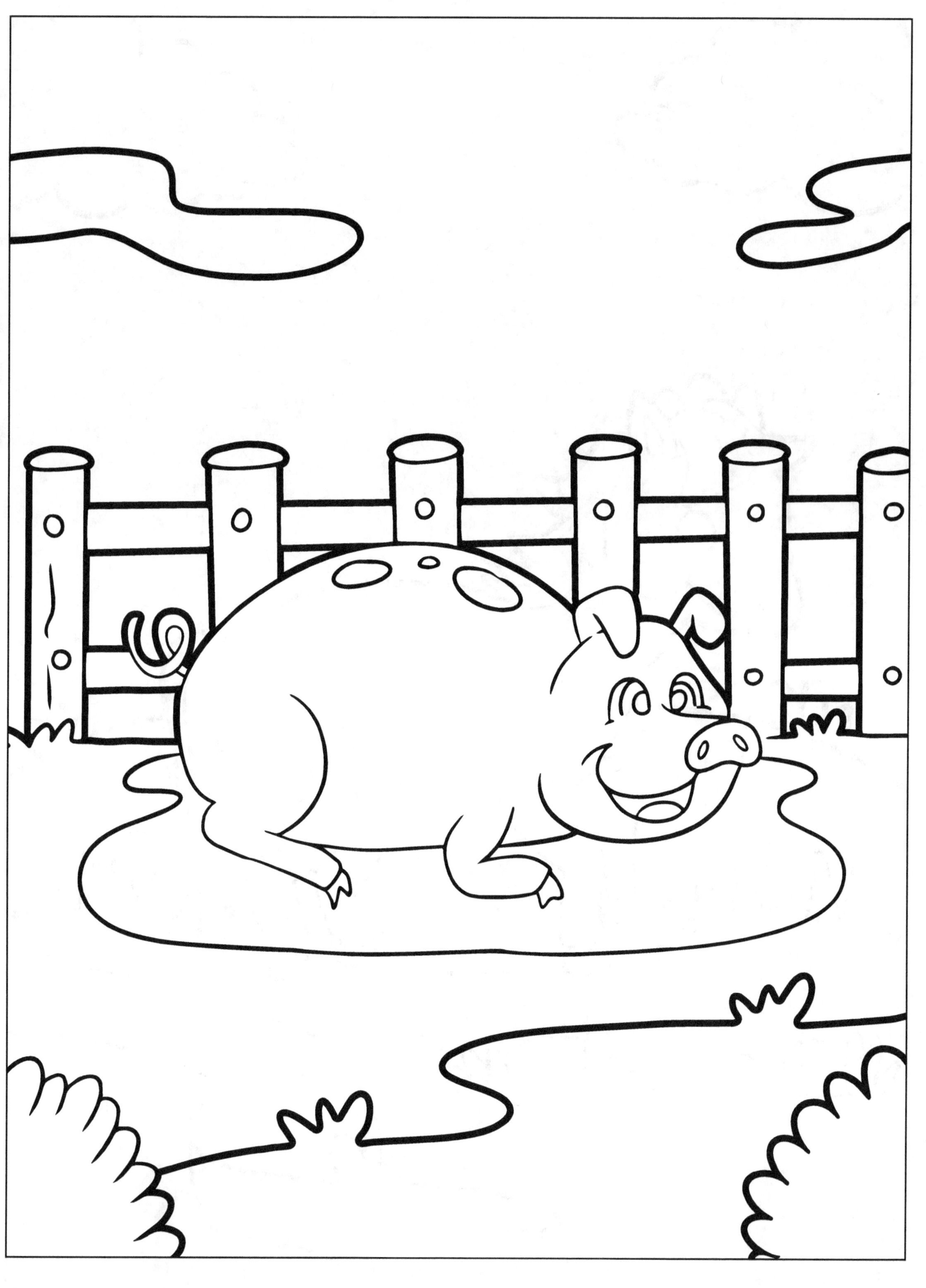

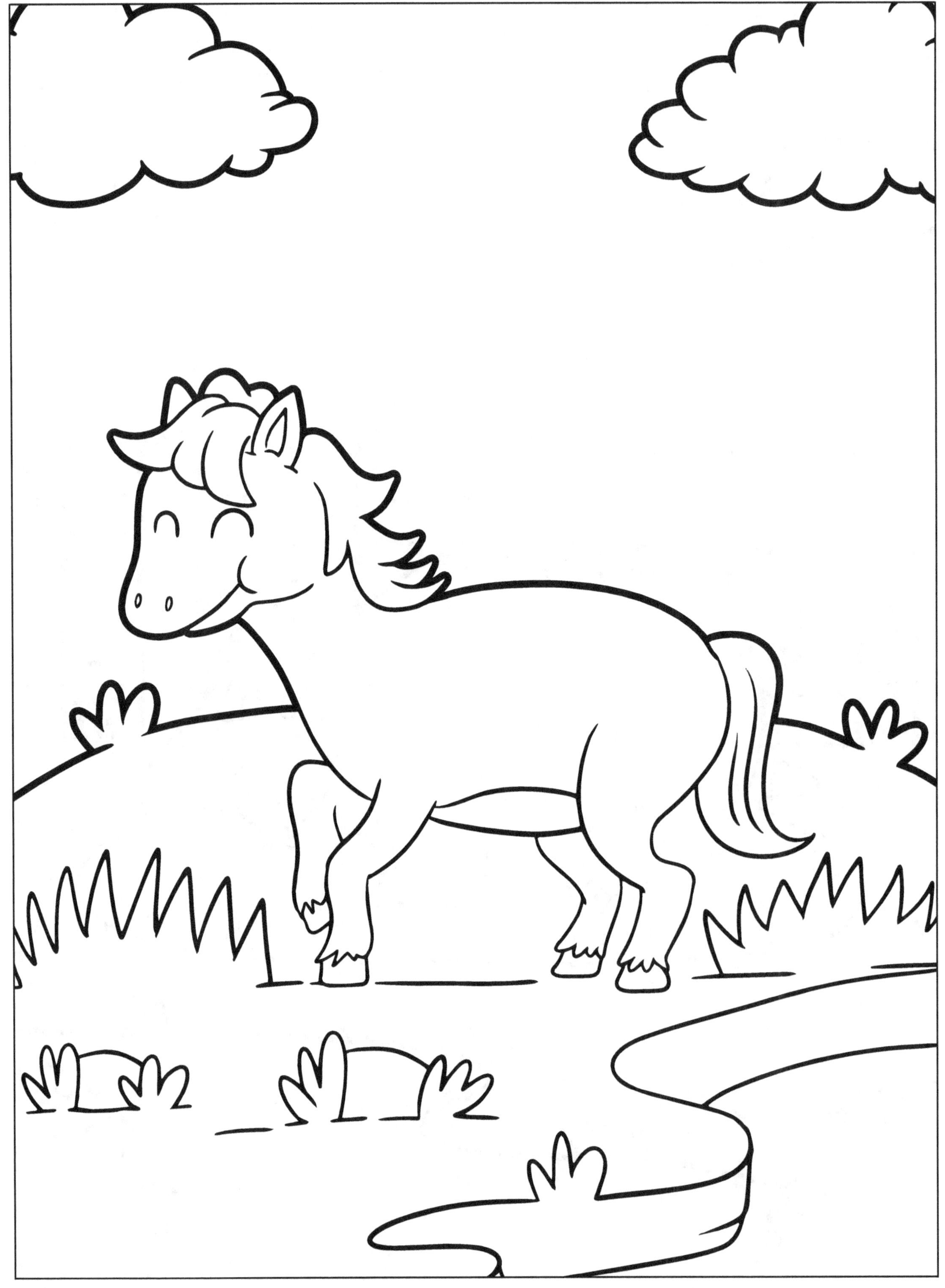

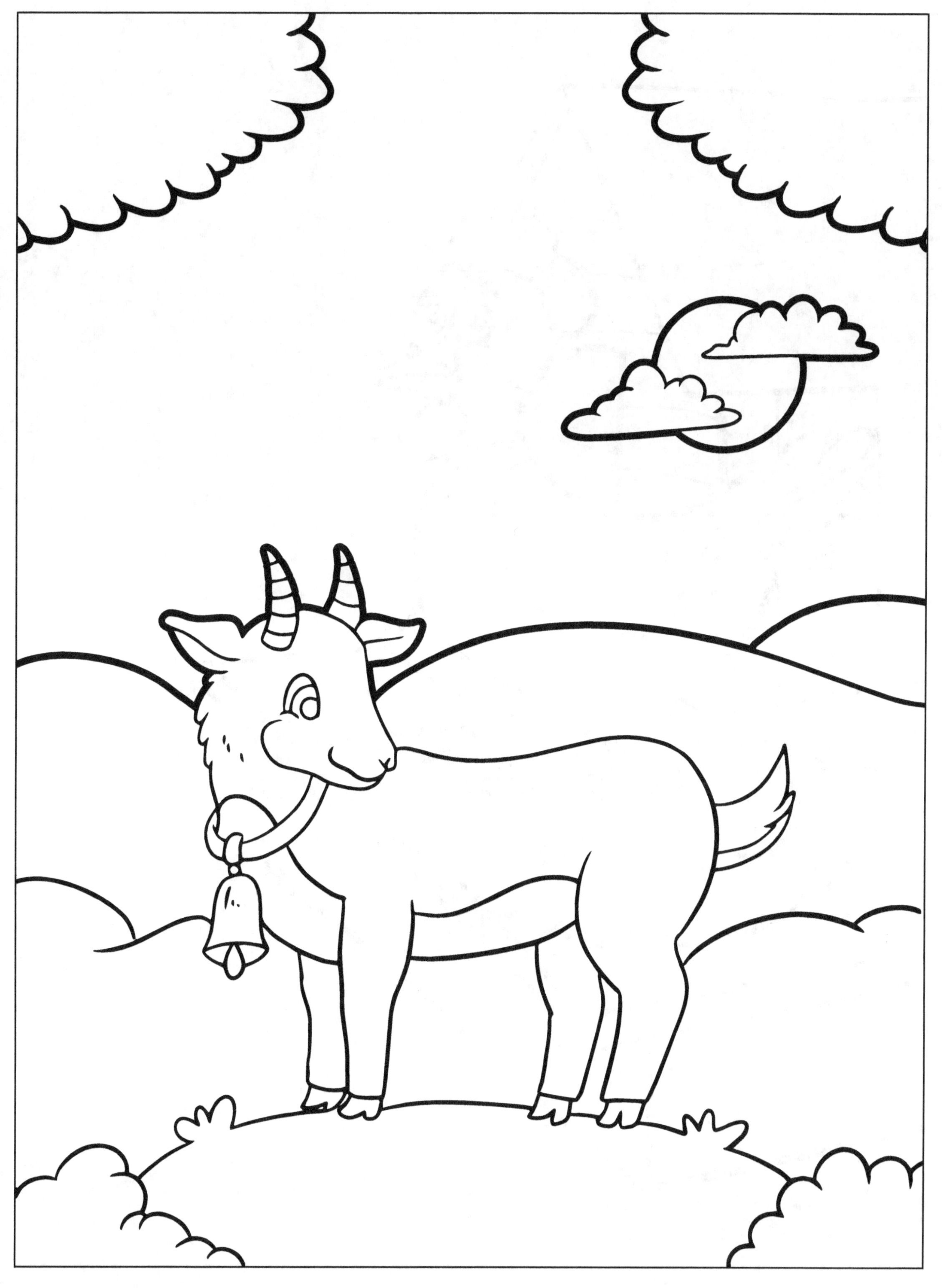

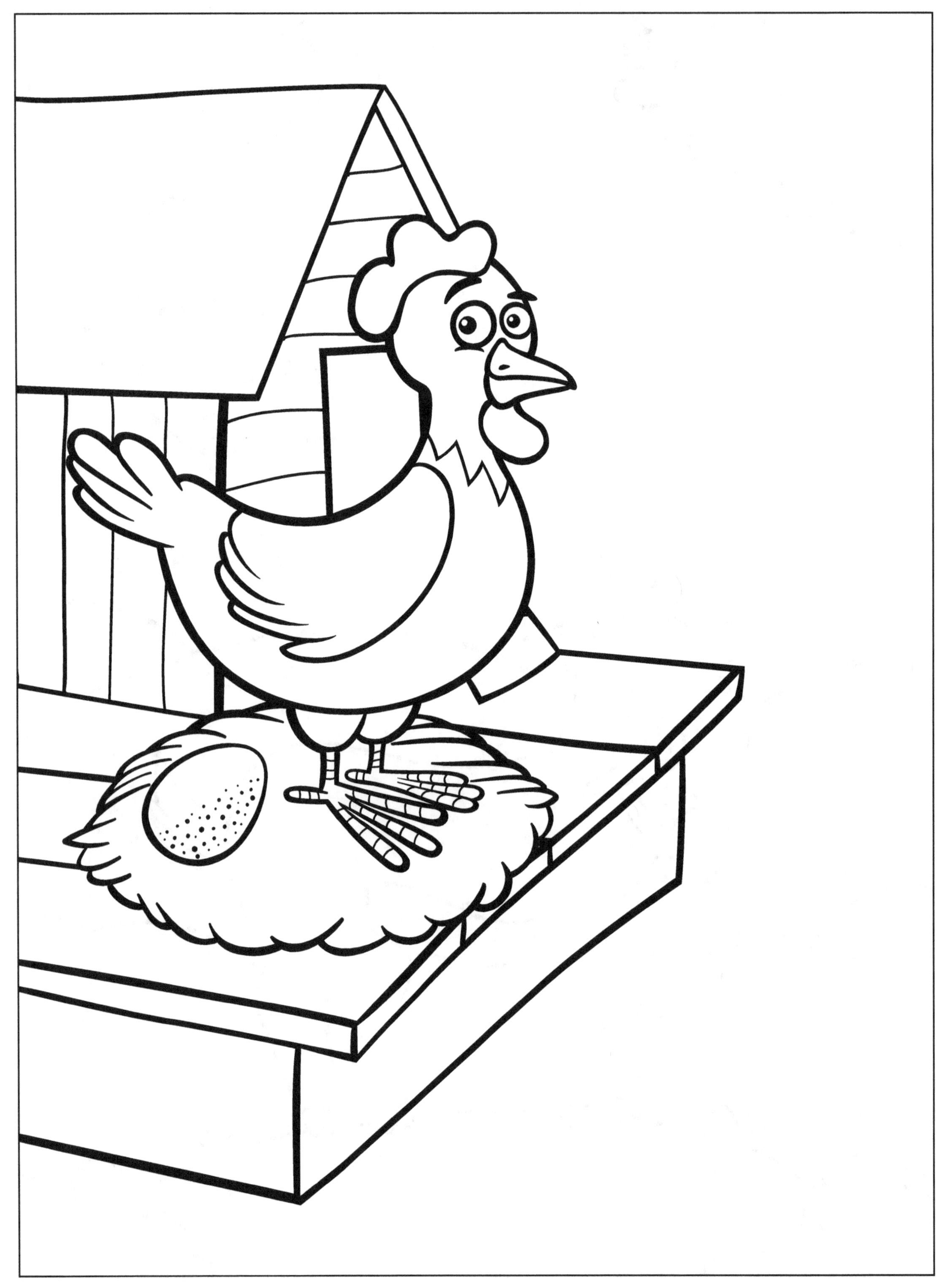

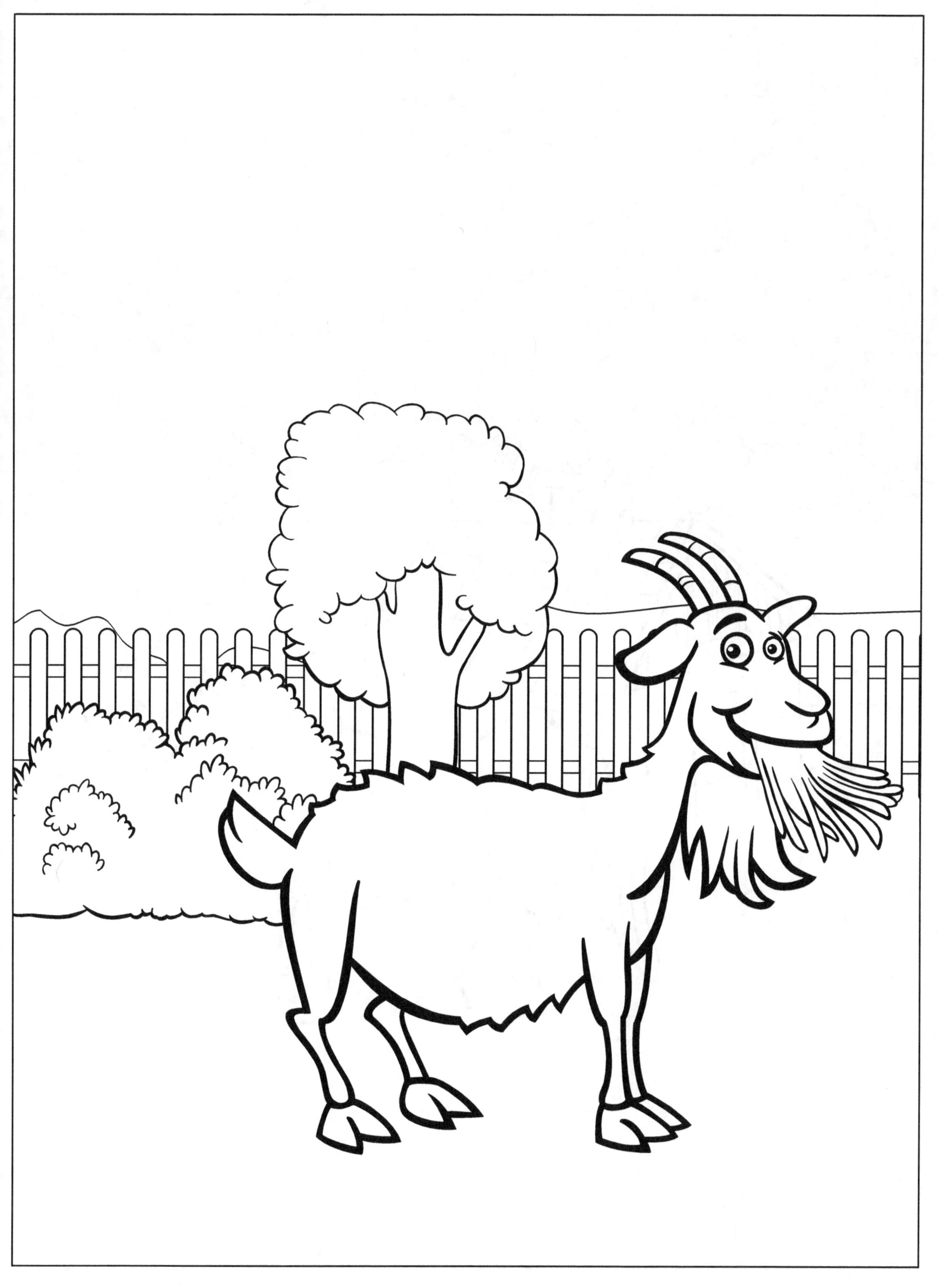

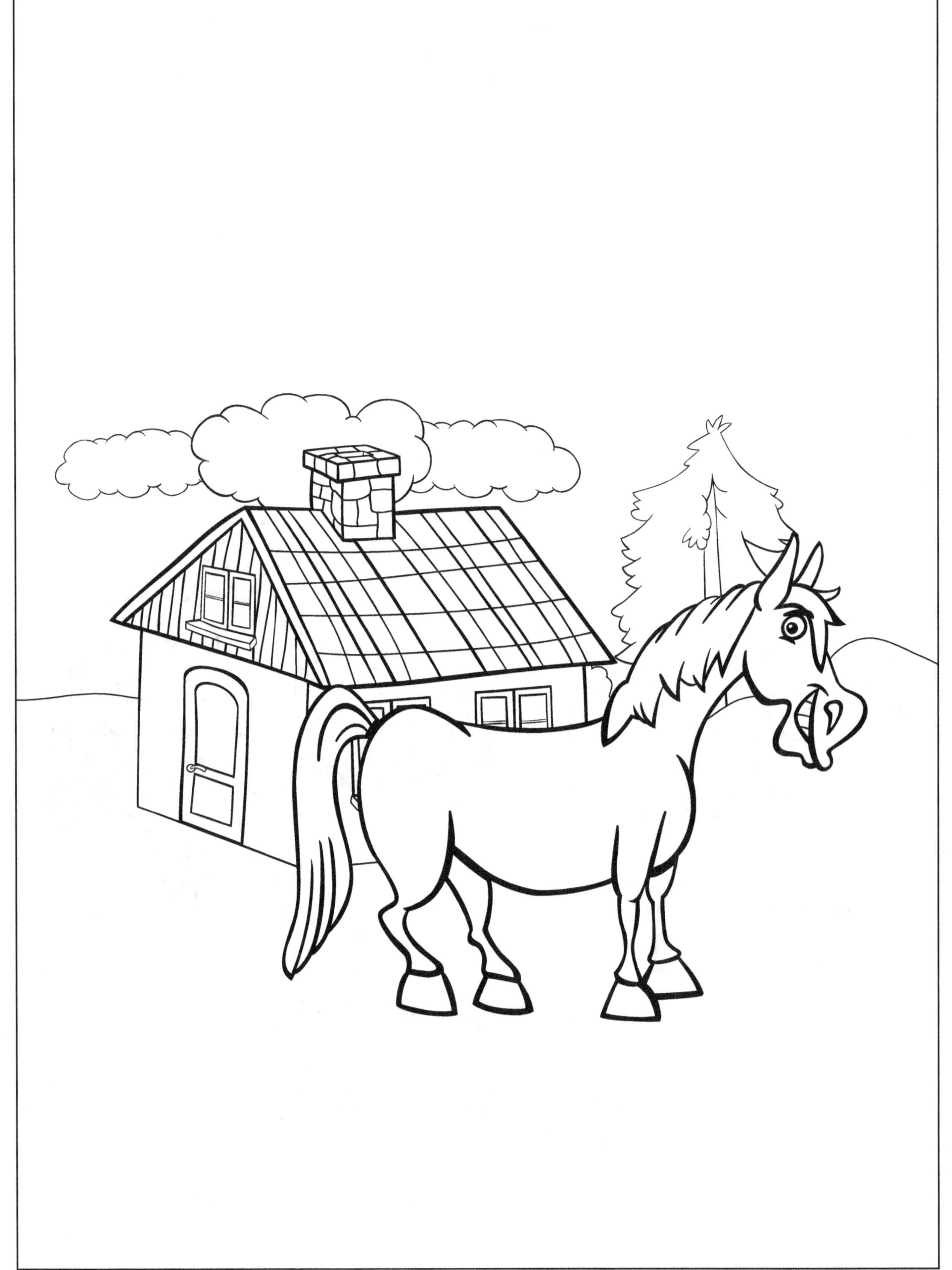

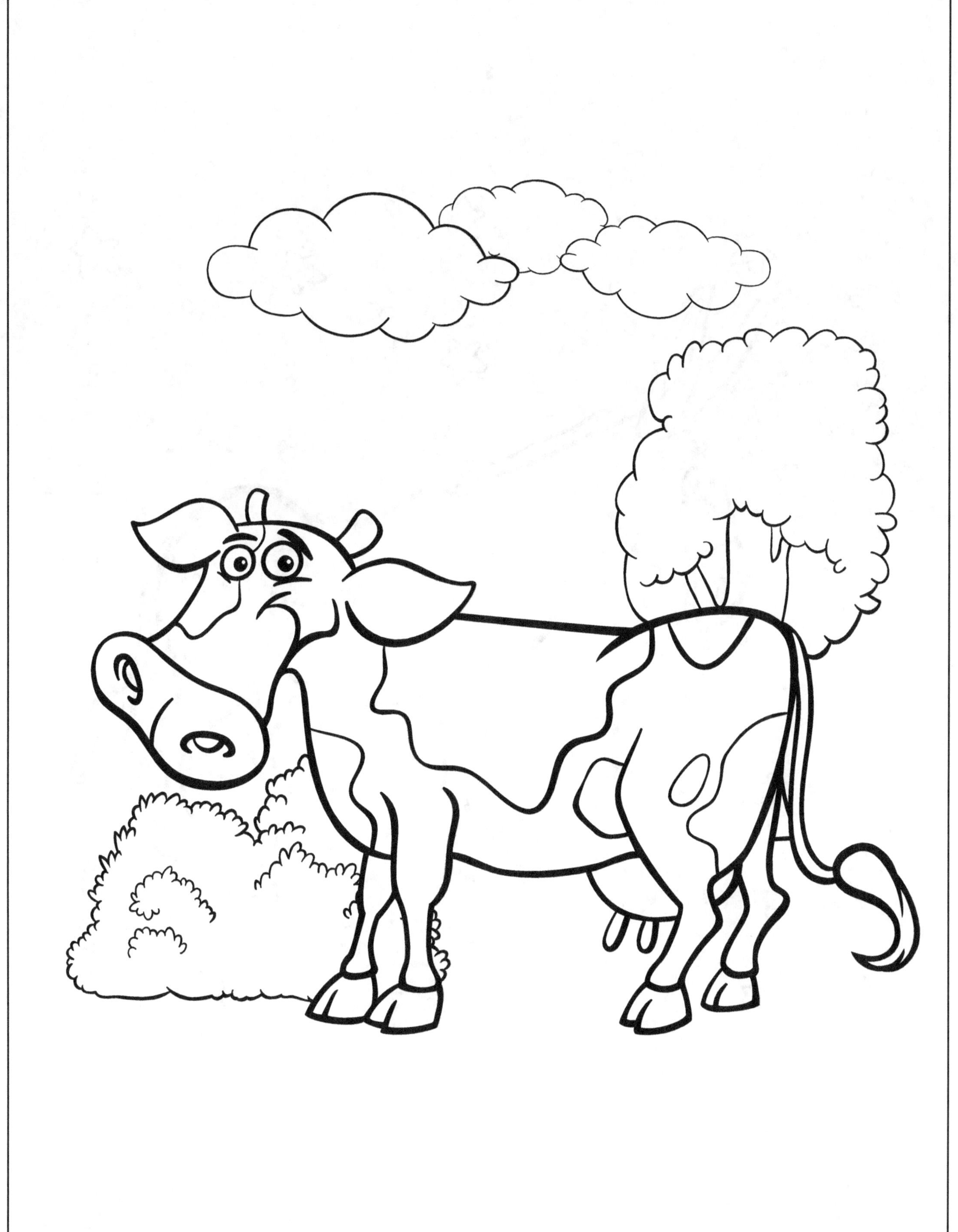

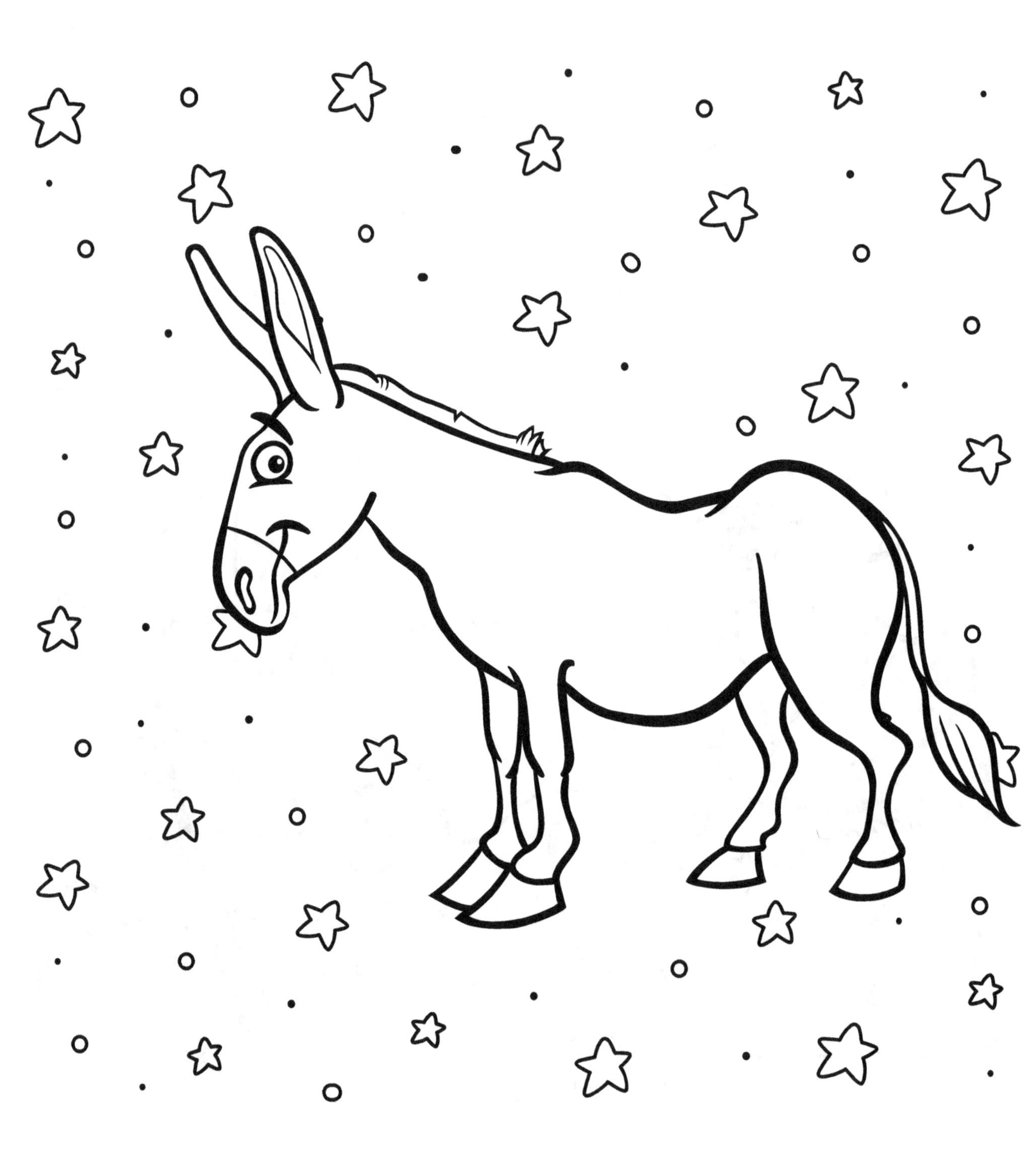

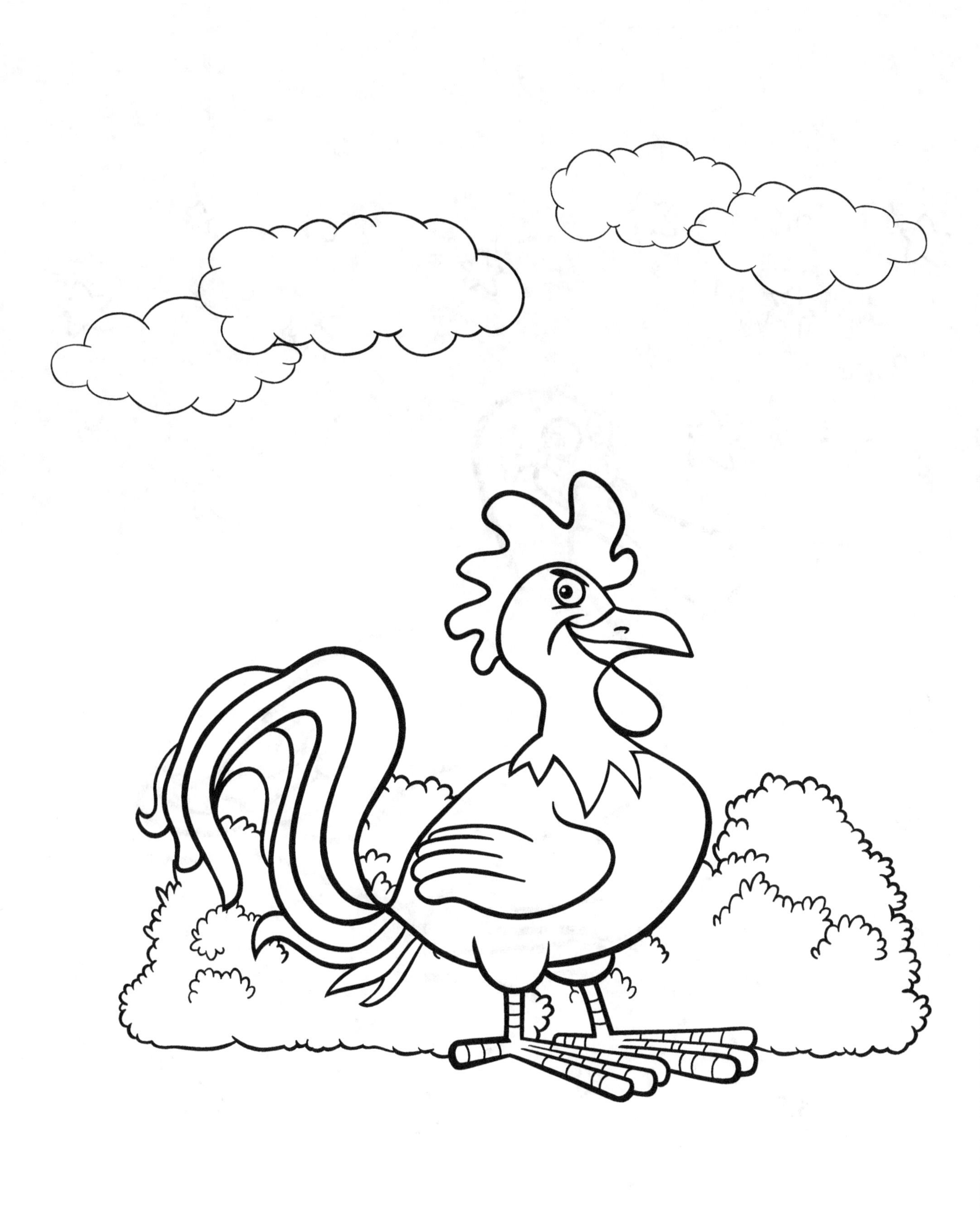

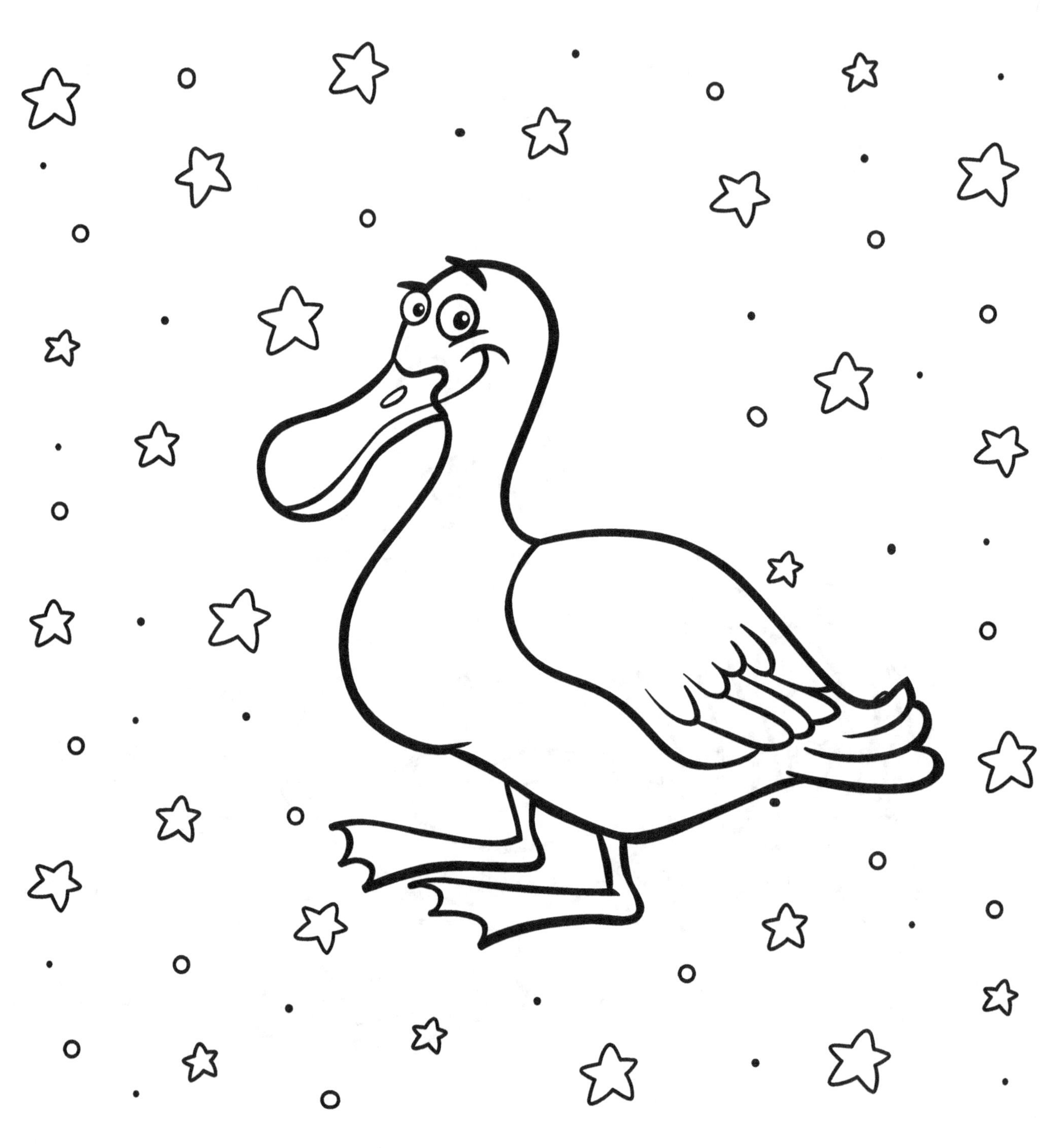

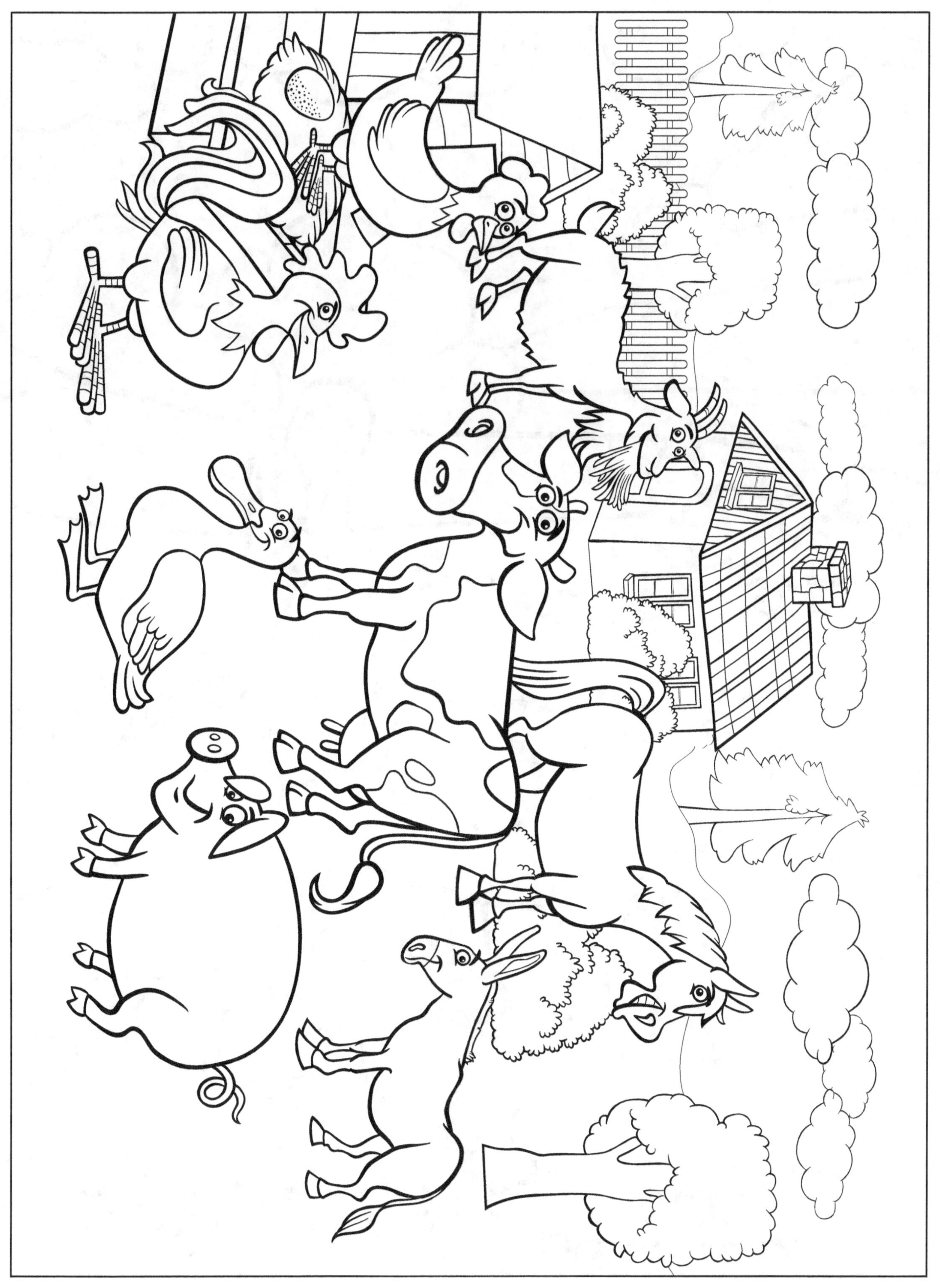

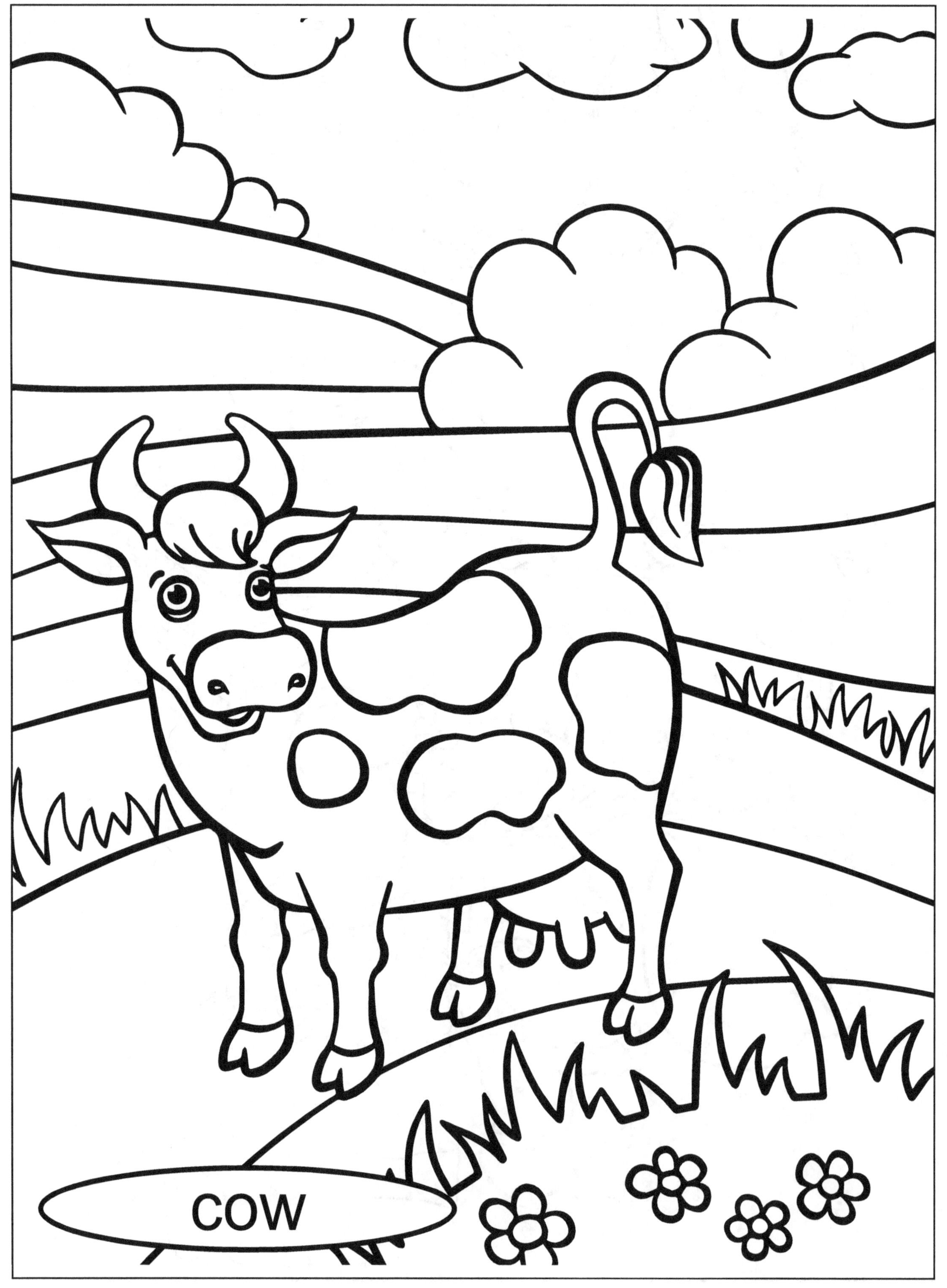

COW

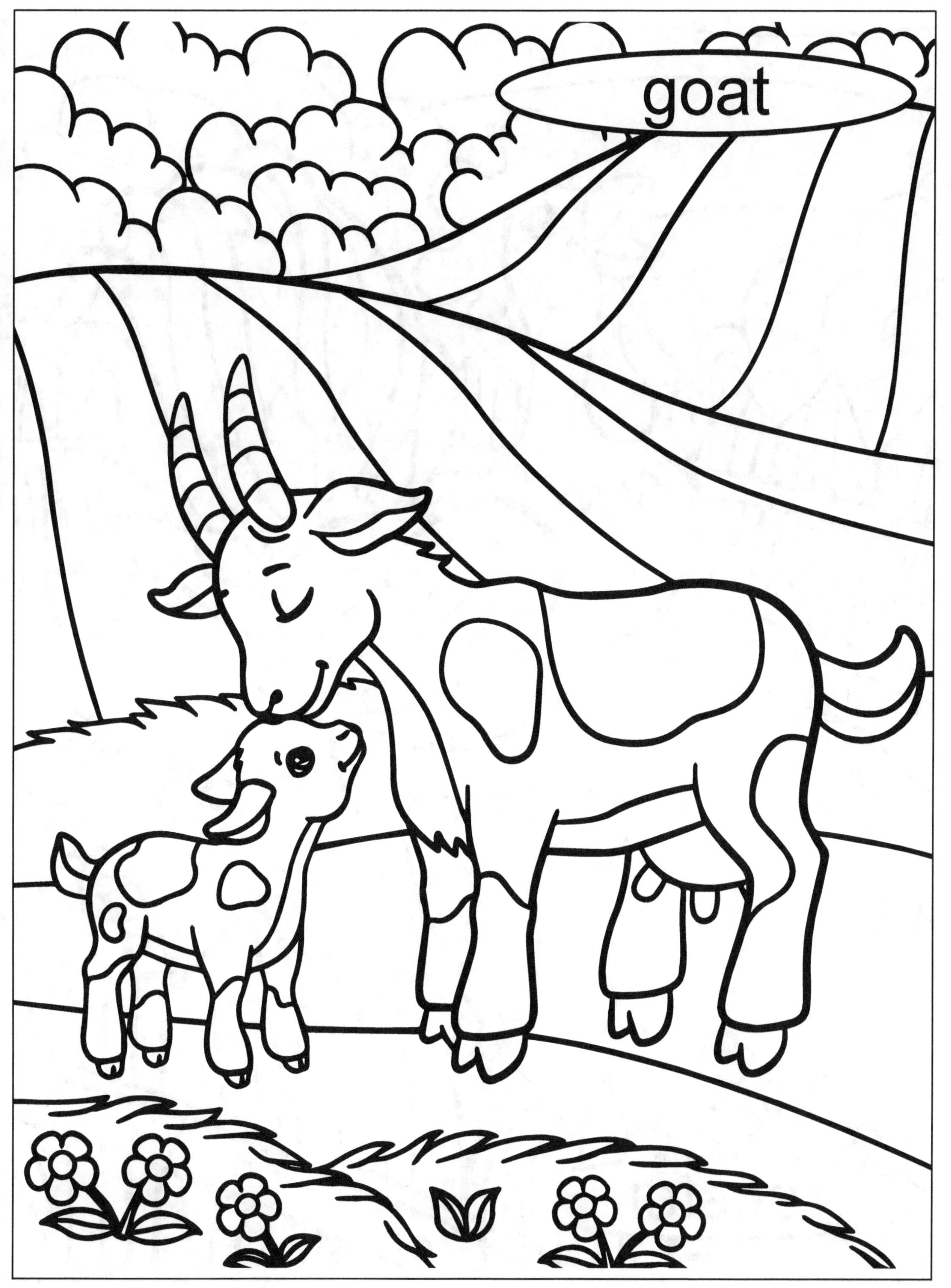

goat

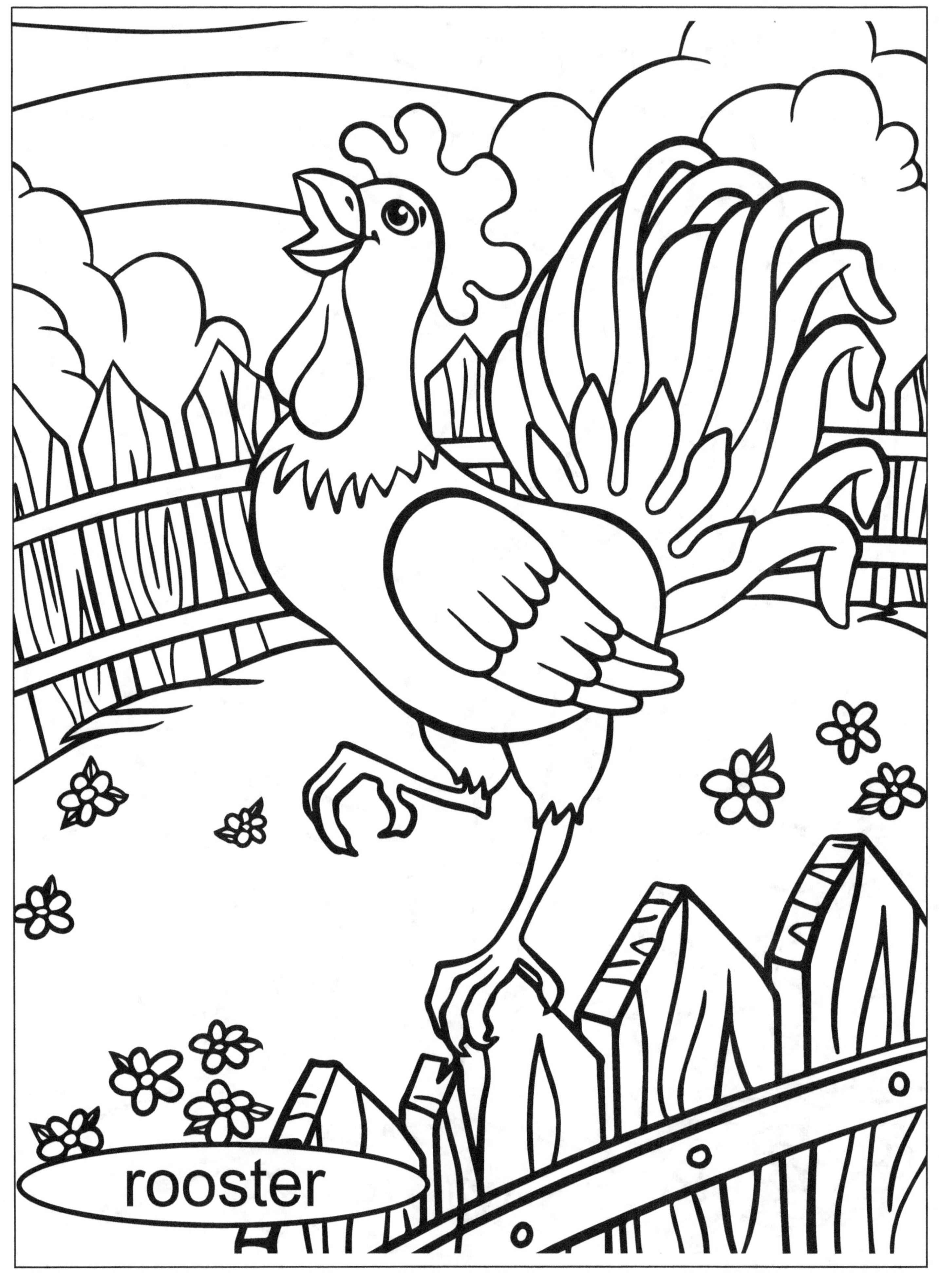
rooster

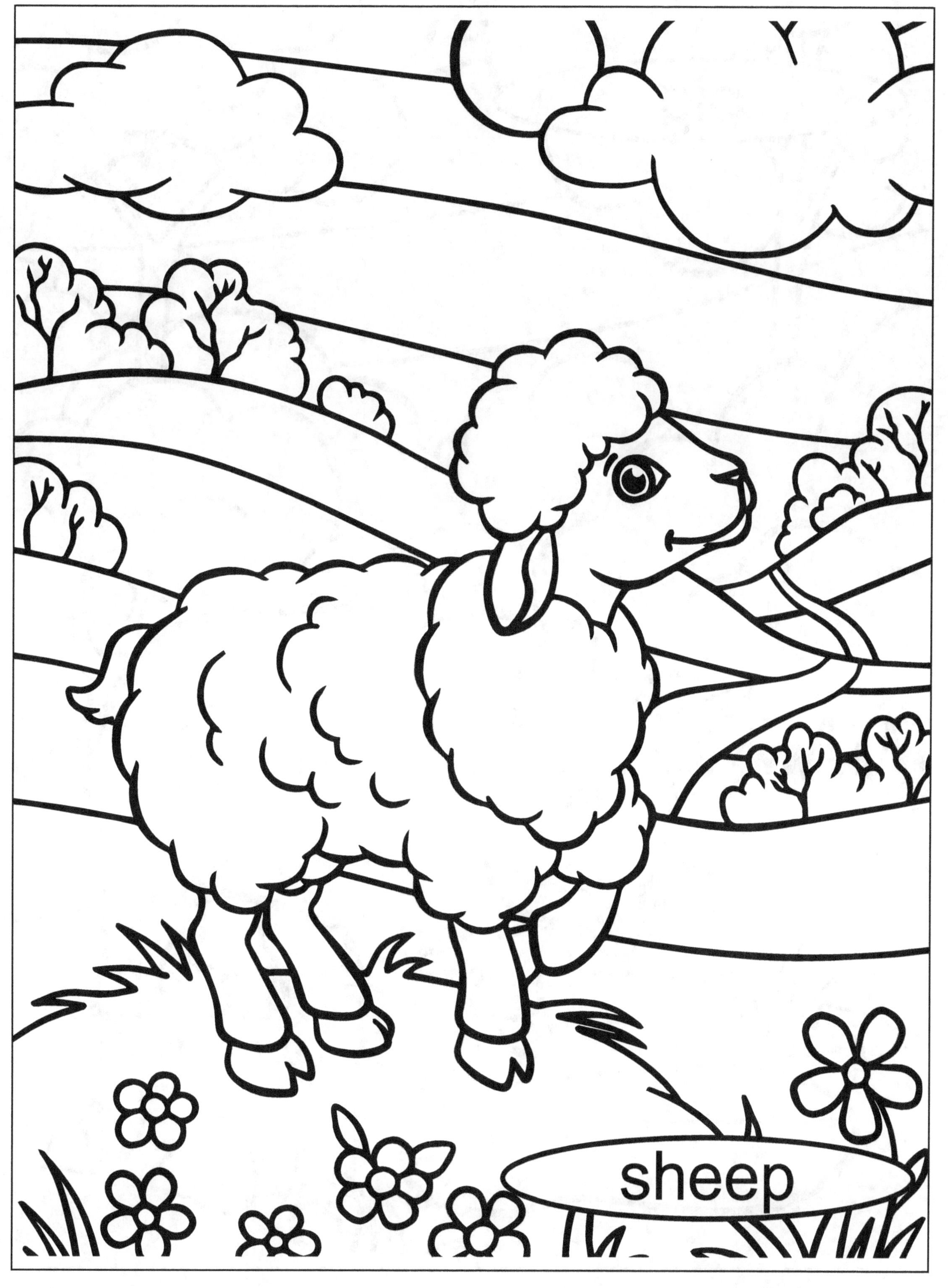
sheep

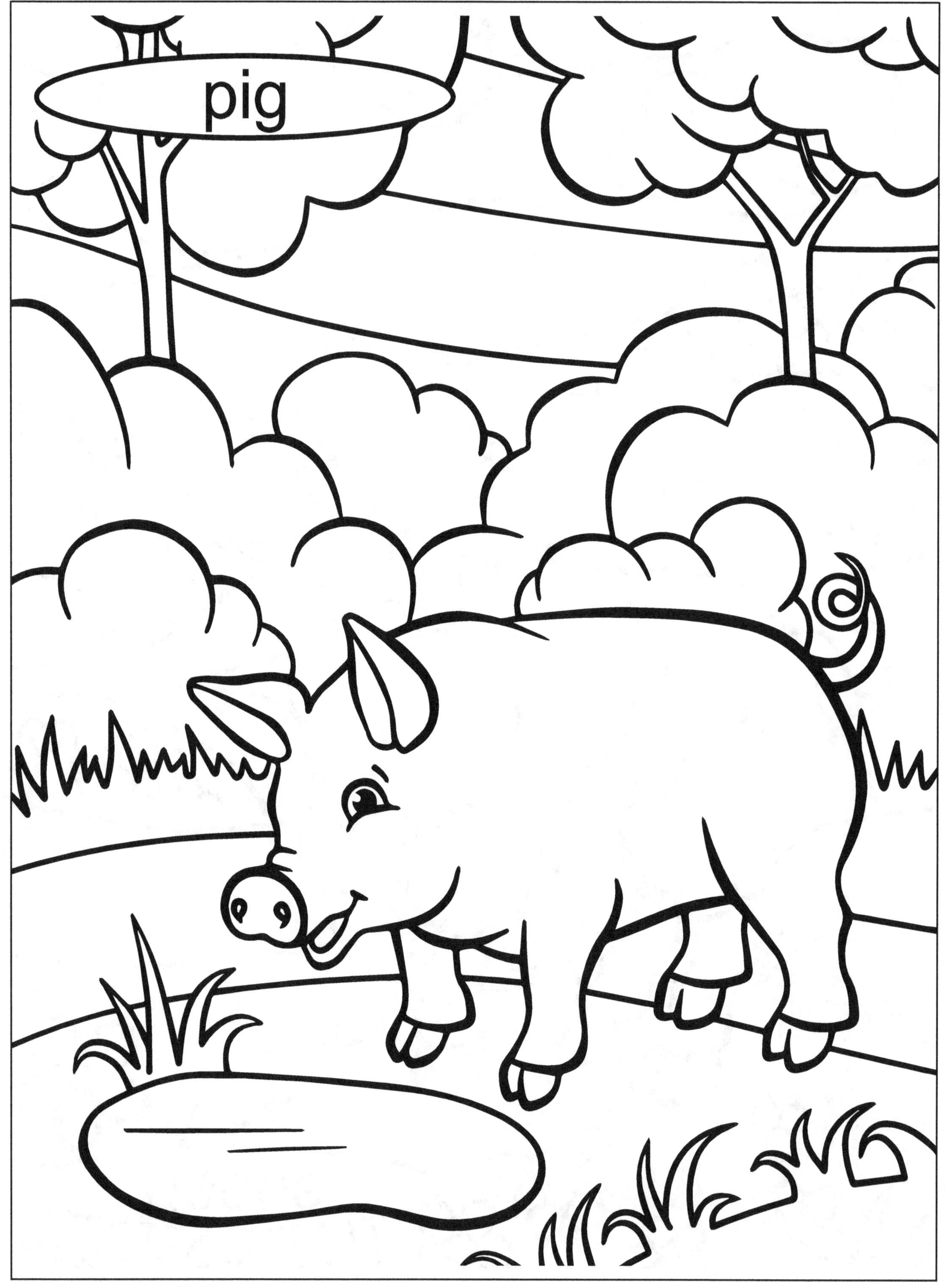

pig

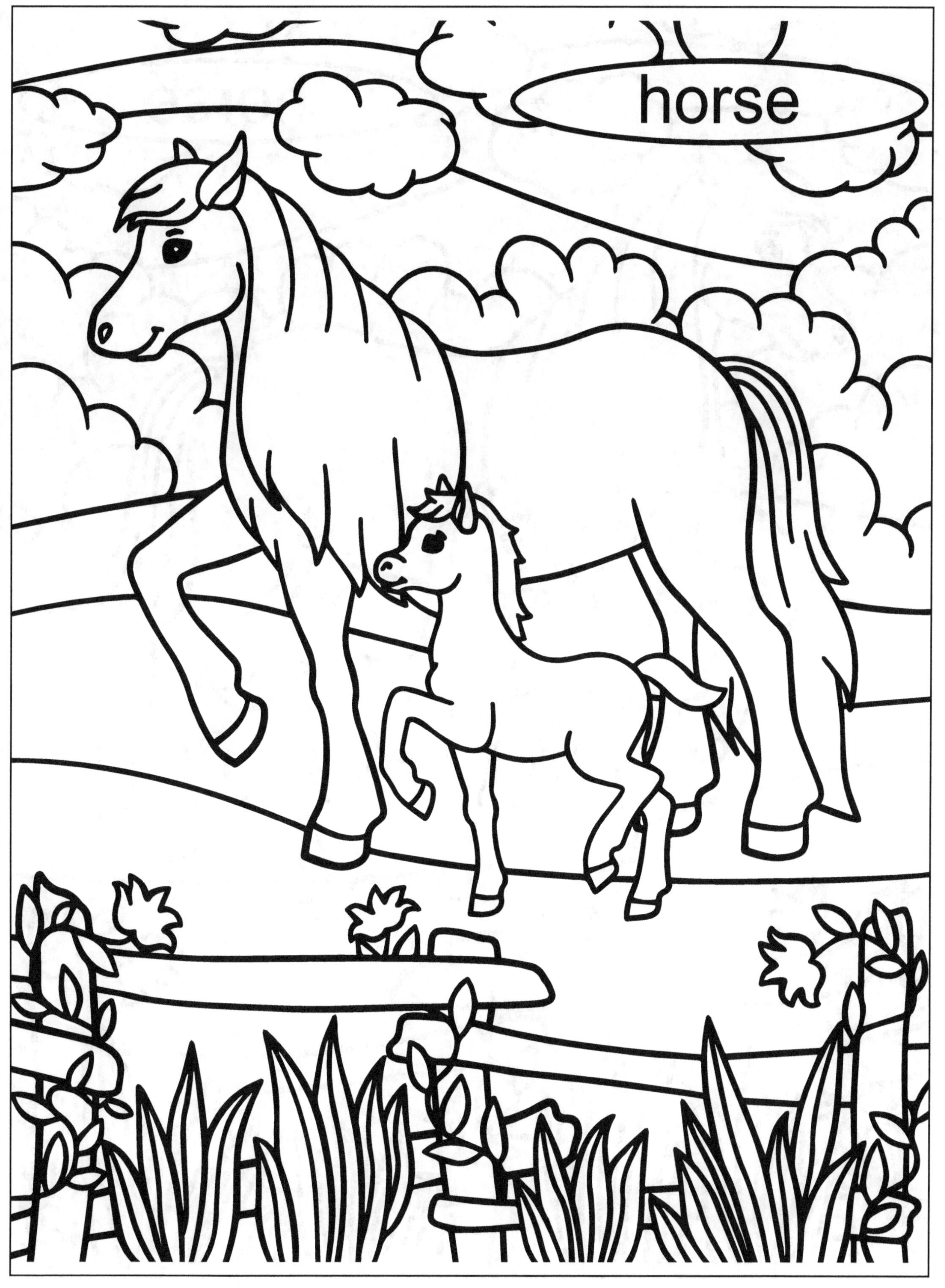
horse

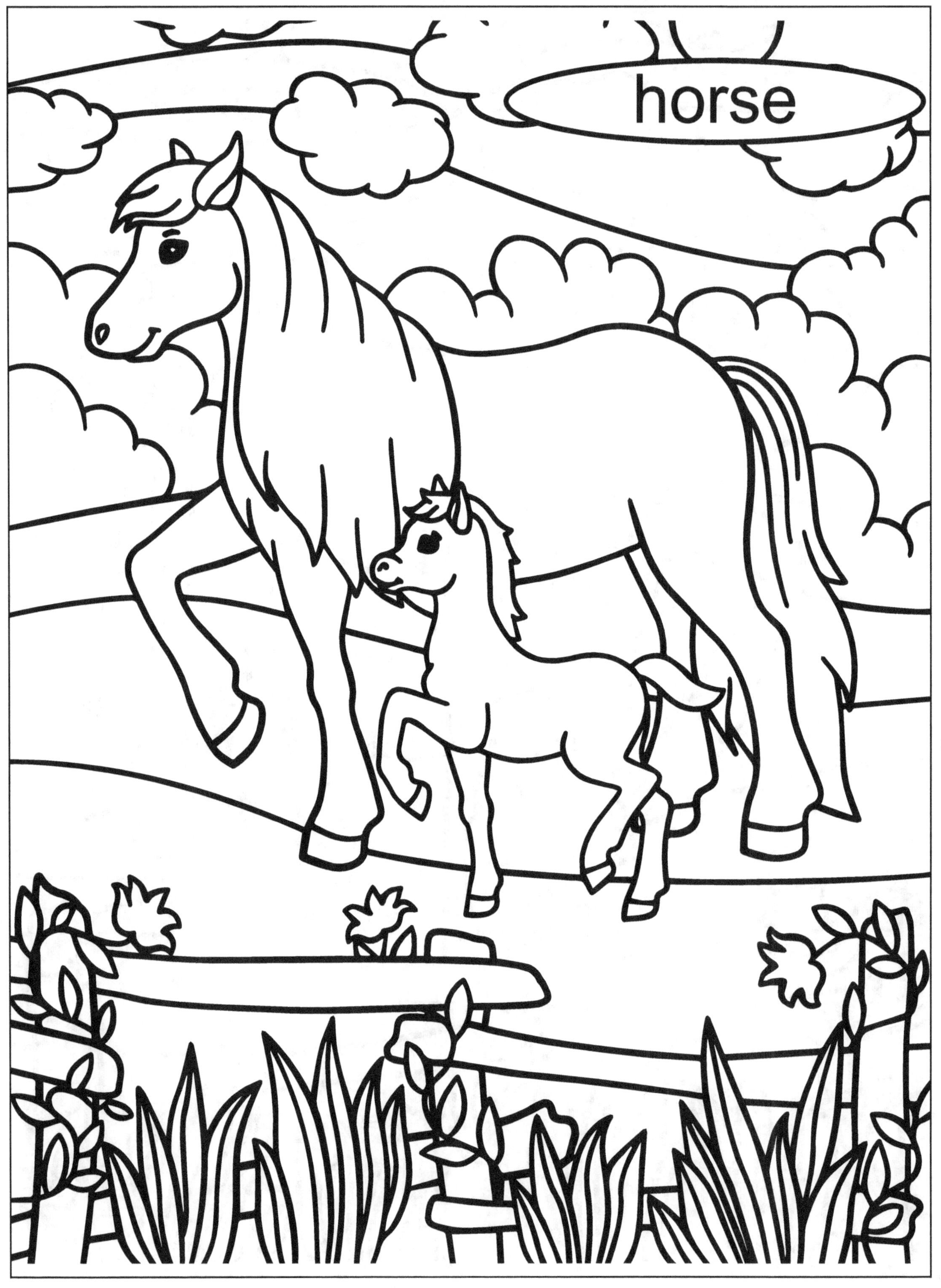
horse

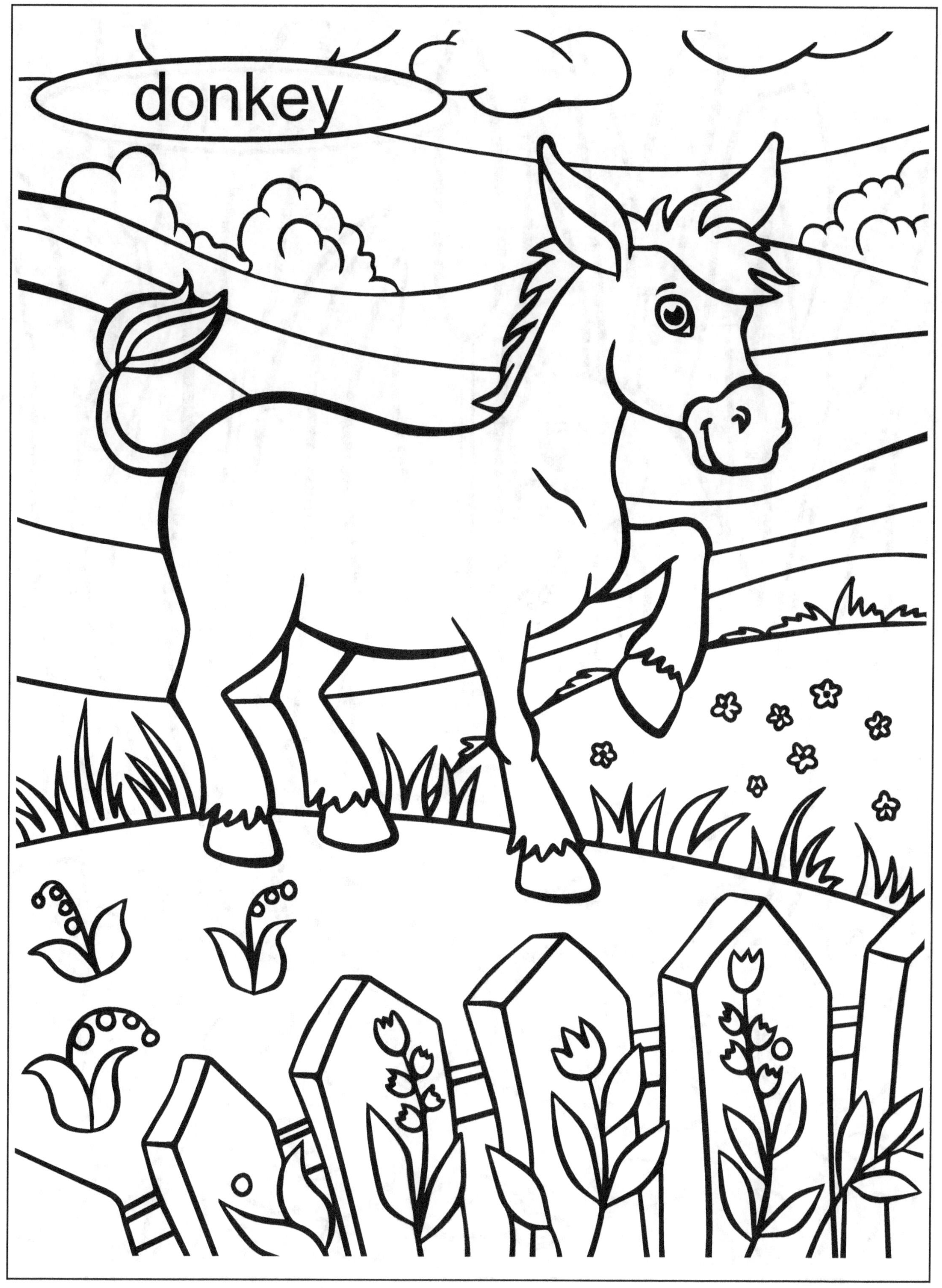
donkey

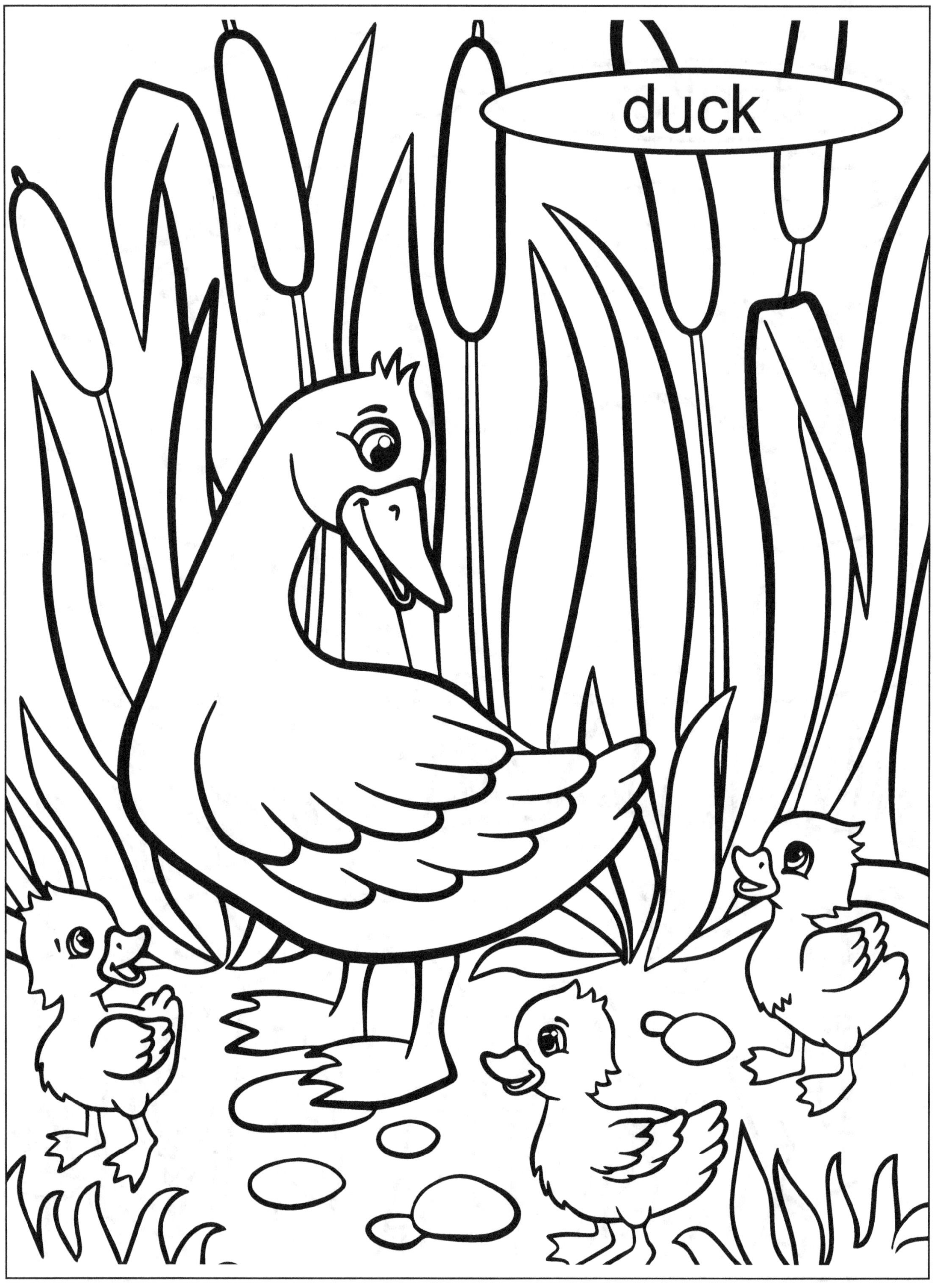

duck